Cubs and Colts and Calves and Kittens

By Allan Fowler

Consultants:
Robert L. Hillerich, Ph.D., Bowling Green
State University, Bowling Green, Ohio

Mary Nalbandian, Director of Science,
Chicago Public Schools, Chicago, Illinois

Fay Robinson, Child Development Specialist

CHILDRENS PRESS®
CHICAGO

Series cover and interior design by Sara Shelton

Library of Congress Cataloging-in-Publication Data

Fowler, Allan.
    Cubs and colts and calves and kittens / by Allan Fowler.
       p.   cm.—(Rookie read-about science)
    Summary: A simple introduction to the physical features and
behavior of a variety of baby animals.
    ISBN 0-516-04913-5
    1. Animals—Infancy—Juvenile literature.   2. Domestic animals—
Infancy—Juvenile literature.   [1. Animals—Infancy.]   I. Title.
II. Series: Fowler, Allan. Rookie read-about science.
QL763.F65   1991
591.3'9—dc20   91-3140
                                                                      CIP
                                                                       AC

When some baby animals are born, their mothers must take care of them just as your mother took care of you.

There are special names
for some baby animals.

You know that baby dogs
are called puppies.

And baby cats are kittens.

Newborn puppies and
kittens can't see or
walk yet.

A baby cow is a calf.

But so is a baby buffalo.

And baby elephants are calves, too.

This young calf has lots of hair. But he will lose most of his hair when he grows up.

Isn't he big for a baby?

But a newborn whale calf can be twice as long as a grown-up elephant!

Young lions and tigers
are called cubs.

Baby bears are also cubs.

This baby horse is a colt.

18

Newborn horses are called foals. This foal is only a few hours old, yet it can walk already.

A baby deer is a fawn.

A baby sheep is a lamb.

A baby pig is a piglet.

See how small these piglets are next to their mother.

All the animals you see in
this book, and many others
like them, are carried
inside their mothers' bodies
before they are born.

When they are very young,
they live on milk from
their mothers.

Some animals have only one baby at a time.

Others have a group of
three or four or even more.
A group of animal babies
is called a litter.

A mother rabbit may give birth to two litters of five bunnies in just one summer.

That's ten bunnies!

How would you like to have so many sisters and brothers?

Words You Know

cubs

colts

calves

kittens

puppies

fawn

lambs

piglets

litter of bunnies

Index

About the Author

Allan Fowler is a free-lance writer with a background in advertising. Born in New York, he lives in Chicago now and enjoys traveling.

Photo Credits

Grant Heilman Photography, Inc.—© Barry L. Runk, 28

Photri—18

SuperStock International, Inc.—Cover

Valan—© J.A. Wilkinson, 5, 6, 15, 27, 31 (top left); © Herman H. Giethoorn, 7, 30 (bottom right); © Val & Alan Wilkinson, 8; © Kennon Cooke, 9, 10; © Jeff Foote, 13; © Stephen J. Krassemann, 14, 20, 25, 30 (bottom left); © Wayne Lankinen, 16; © Pam E. Hickman, 17, 30 (top right); © A.B. Joyce, 21, 31 (center left); © Francis Lépine, 23; © B. Lyon, 26; © Robert C. Simpson, 30 (top left); © Murray O'Neill, 31 (top right); © V. Whelan, 31 (center right); © Harold V. Green, 31 (bottom)

COVER: Baby animals on a bench